Quotes on World Peace from World Leaders

Anti-Accentism

DR. EMMANUELADETULA

Center for Peace
Christ Channel Network

ABOUTCCNCENTERFORPEACE

CCN Center for Peace is a division of Christ Channel Network (CCN); Christ Channel is a bona fide 501(c) (3) nonprofit organizationin the United States founded in 2002 by Rev. Dr. Emmanuel Adetula.

Toorderadditionalcopiesofthisbook:

Write to: CHRIST CHANNEL NETWORK INC.

Mailing: P.O. BOX 1017 Lawndale,CA.90260   USA

E-Mail: tulatax2015@gmail.com

Christ Channel Network Inc.
www.christchannelnetwork.org

How beautiful upon the mountains are the feet of him who brings good tidings, who publishespeace.
—**Isaiah52:7**

Emmanuel Adetula

Mahatma Gandhi

CESAR CHAVEZ

Gil Bailie

Martin Luther King Jr.

Nelson Mandela

Oscar Arias

Joan Baez

Stanley Baldwin

Thomas Aquinas

Mother Teresa

ACKNOWLEDGMENTS

CCN Center Peace is an organization whose mission is to seek and pursue good governments, religious peace, liberty, non-violence and social justice around the world theorganization promotes the rule of law, transitional justice, and democracy and features interviews and dialogues with political and religious leaders, as well as the academic community. The result of these dialogues and interviews produced excellent cross-cultural ideas and statements across the board, our programs resulted in the creation of quotes of world leaders as produced in this book. Therefore, it should be noted by the readers that the book contains a lot of lifted matters not in the correct format (e.g., use of double quotation marks, citation of sources) for quoted materials. The quotations are not the accurate reproductions of the original. Therefore, it may appear to be with inconsistencies in interpolations since it did not carry the wording, spelling, capitalization, and internal punctuation of the original.

If we have no peace, it is because we have forgotten that we **BELONG** to each other. Mother Teresa

Mother Teresa

Genius is one % inspiration and ninety-nine % perspiration.
--Thomas Edison

Thomas Edison

Dalai Lama

The Dalai Lama, when asked what surprised him most about humanity, answer "Man. Because he sacrifices his health in order to make money. Then he sacrifices money to recuperate his health. And then he is so anxious about the future that he does not enjoy the present; the result being that he does not live in the present or the future; he lives as if he is never going to die, and then he dies having never really lived."

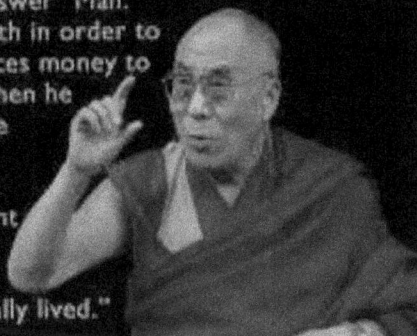

Quotes on World Peace from WorldLeaders

We must build dikes of courage to hold back the flood of fear . . . That old law about "an eye for an eye" leaves everybody blind . . . The time is always right to do the right thing . . . Peace is not merely a distant goal that we seek, but a means by which we arrive at that goal.
—Dr. Martin Luther KingJr.

My generation will be the last in this world to disagree that the succor which is given this world from America is not itself something to rejoice at greatly, But I also say that I can see more in the knowledge that America is going to win a right to continue to be at the world conference table when the terms of peace are discussed in the new world order that is now in the making , It would have been a tragedy for mankind if America had not been put there by God in a times like this, with all the influence and super power, history has thought us that Empires , powerful nations and kings will behave wisely once they have exhausted all the other alternatives and options on the table.

------Dr. Emmanuel Adetula

The only real security is not insurance or money or a job, not a house and furniture paid for, or a retirement fund, and never is it another person. It is the skill and humor and courage within, the ability to build your own fires and find your ownpeace.
—AudreySutherland

When someone steals another's clothes, we call them a thief. Should we not give the same name to one who could clothe the naked and does not? The bread in your cupboard belongs to the hungry; the coat unused in your closet belongs to the one who needs it; the shoes rotting in your closet belong to the one who has no shoes; the money which you hoard up belongs to the poor. **—Basil theGreat**

Holding on to anger is like grasping a hot coal with the intent of throwing it at someone else; you are the one gettingburned.
—**Buddha**

Teach this triple truth to all: A generous heart, kind speech, and a life of service and compassion are the things which renewhumanity.
—**Buddha**

Non-violence, which is the quality of the heart, cannot come by an appeal to thebrain.
—**CesarChavez**

The first principle of non-violent action is that of non-cooperation with everythinghumiliating.
—**CesarChavez**

The non-violent technique does not depend for its success on the goodwill of the oppressor, but rather on the unfailing assistance of God.
—**CesarChavez**

Non-violence is not inaction. It is not discussion. It is not for the timid or weak . . . Non-violence is hard work. It is the willingness to sacrifice. It is the patience towin.
—**CesarChavez**

Violence just hurts those who are already hurt . . . Instead of exposing the brutality of the oppressor, it justifiesit.
—**CesarChavez**

We are convinced that non-violence is more powerful than violence. We are convinced that non-violence supports you if you have a just and moral cause . . . If you use violence, you have to sell part of yourself for that violence. Then you are no longer a master of your ownstruggle.
—**CesarChavez**

There is no such thing as defeat innon-violence.
—**CesarChavez**

You know, if people are not pacifists, it's not their fault. It's because society puts them in that spot. You've got to change it. You don't just change a man—you've got to change his environment as you do it.
—**CesarChavez**

Through Gandhi and my own life experience, I have learned about nonviolence. I believe that human life is a very special gift from God, and that no one has a right to take that away in any cause, however just. I am convinced that nonviolence is more powerful thanviolence.
—**CesarChavez**

Non-violence exacts a very high price from one who practices it. But once you are able to meet that demand then you can do mostthings.
—**CesarChavez**

Non-violence is a very powerful weapon. Most people don't understand the power of non-violence and tend to be amazed by the whole idea. Those who have been involved in bringing about change and see the difference between violence and non-violence are firmly committed to a lifetime of non-violence, not because it is easy or because it is cowardly, but because it is an effective and very powerfulway -----**Cesar Chavez**

Youth is the first victim of war; the first fruit of peace. It takes 20 years or more of peace to make a man; it takes only 20 seconds of war to destroyhim.
—**Baudouin I, King ofBelgium**

No man is an island entire of itself . . . any man's death diminishes me because I am involved in mankind; and therefore never send to know for whom the bell tolls; it tolls forthee.
—**JohnDonne**

The bomb that fell on Hiroshima fell on America,too.
—**HermannHagedorn**

Peace comes from being able to contribute the best that we have, and all that we are, toward creating a world that supports everyone. But it is also securing the space for others to contribute the best that they have and all that theyare.
—**HafsatAbiola**

The good we secure for ourselves is precarious and uncertain until it is secured for all of us and incorporated into our commonlife.
—**JaneAddams**

The etymology of the term *anti-Semitism* is a special case of prejudice, hatred, or persecution directed against people who are in some way different from the rest—for example, a case of prejudice, hatred, or persecution directed against certain people of different accent from your own ethnic group's or nationality's. Semitism means people with a Semitic language like the Jews or Arabs or Ibo orYoruba.
Dr. Emmanuel Adetula

No matter how big a nation is, it is no stronger that it's weakest people, and as long as you keep a person down, some part of you has to be down there to hold him down, so it means you cannot soar as you might otherwise **(MarianAnderson).**

If you have prejudice against someone because of race, you are called a racist, but if you have prejudice against someone because of their accent, you are then anti-Semitic. Though the Jews have taken the word only to describe their own history for political agenda, the truth remains that the foundation of anti-Semitism is anti-accents or anti-people with difficult to understandlanguage.Until lions have their historians, tales of the hunt shall always glorify the hunters

The foundation of every genocide is simply ethnic cleansing. That is a situation where you want to wipe out certain people of the same ethnic group from the larger society. In human history, the way you recognize those of an ethnic origin is never the way they look but by the way of pronunciation of certain words. Accents were used to identify some Jews sixty-two years ago by the Nazis, the same way accents were used to carry out the genocide of eight hundred thousand Rwandans within ten days, so there cannot be a successful genocide without identification by an accent.

Dr. Emmanuel Adetula

Barak Obama

With my accent, you can guess my nationality just by listening to the sound of my voice, and if you already have a prejudice against my national or ethnic origin, the possibility for you to naturally develop hatred or persecution or suspicion or lack of trust or stereotype toward me may not be far-fetched because if you define my English language with the standard pronunciation of your own and you let my accent make you lose interest in what I may have say, you probably may end up placing a lesser value on me and end up seeing me as a liability to you rather than an asset to your community, which automatically will put you in a position to lose the benefits of my talents and gifts to your world—all because you did not receive me for the simple fact that I speak English language with a low, acceptable, standard pronunciation that is not pleasing and sweet to your hearing with excellency of speech, so the next thing you want may be to shut me out, so anti-Semitism emanated from anti-accent.

Dr. Emmanuel Adetula

A solid rock is not disturbed by the wind; even so, a wise person is not agitated by praise or blame**(Dhammapada).**

We should take care in inculcating patriotism into our boys and girls—that is, patriotism above the narrow sentiment—which usually stops at one's country and thus inspires jealousy and enmity in dealing with others . . . Our patriotism should be of the wider, nobler kind that recognizes justice and reasonableness in the claims of others and that leads our country into comradeship with other nations of the world. The first step to this end is to develop peace and goodwill within our borders by training our youth of both sexes to its practice as their habit of life, so that the jealousies of town against town, class against class, sect against sect, and race against race no longer exist and then to extend this good feeling beyond our frontiers toward our neighbors **(LordBaden-Powell).**

The greatest fear and complain of biblical prophets including Moses and Apostle Paul in their conversation concerning the call of God as leaders of the people was about their possible rejection by the world due to their lack of acceptable standard pronunciation of spoken words with an excellent speech that will be pleasing to the people of their generation. **(EMMANUELADETULA)**

I will advise you not to listen to my accent but to my arguments, which are plain and unlearned except in the school of sound common sense under the influence of Christian principles. My arguments are with a force that the learning and talent of the people of this world cannot gainsay or resist. I have truth on my side; though my statements, actions, and writings are dressed in a humble garb, they are mightier than error though clothed with the brilliancy of imagination, the pomp of declamation, and the cunning of sophistry. God hath chosen me the weak thing of this world, who cannot boast of my birth and pedigree, of my ancient and illustrious family, who have no titles of honor to aggrandize me nor estates, possessions, and worldly substance to support myself with. I will, by the deliberate and free action of God's gracious will, confound the things that are mighty in this planet.

(EMMANUEL ADETULA)

In Shemoth Rabba, sec. 17, fol. 117, it is said: "There are certain matters which appear little to men, yet by them God points out important precepts." Instead, God chose things the world considers foolish in order to shame those who think they are wise. And 1 Corinthians 1:27 says that God chose things that are powerless to shame those who are powerful. God chose me because he best judges what men are in their heart. I have not come to you with excellency of speech but with wisdom, power, and truth that come from a sound mind to establish a new world order where liberty and freedom shall reign. **(EMMANUELADETULA)**

The love of one's country is a splendid thing. But why should love stop at the border? **(PabloCasals).**

The hottest places in hell are reserved for those who, in times of great moral crisis, maintain their neutrality because they don't want be themselves but want to be like everybody**(Dante).**

Making mendacious, dehumanizing, demonizing, or stereotypical allegations about persons because of their accent is over-the-top of **our already existing problem of racism in our society. (EMMANUELADETULA)**

When prejudice denies someone a job or a contract that he or she is qualified to obtain in a multicultural society just like Adolf Hitler did to German and European Jews sixty-two years ago, it is then qualified to compare anti-Semitism at same level withantia-ccentism.

(EMMANUELADETULA)

When evil is allowed to compete with good, evil has an emotional populist appeal that wins out unless good men and women stand as a vanguard againstabuse.
—Hannah Arendt

The sad truth is that most evil is done by people who never make up their minds to be good orevil.
—Hannah Arendt

Peace is not the product of a victory or a command. It has no finishing line, no final deadline, and no fixed definition of achievement. Peace is a never-ending process, the work of manydecisions.
—**OscarArias**

In the absence of justice, what is sovereignty but organizedrobbery?
—**St.Augustine**

That's all nonviolence is—organizedlove.
—**JoanBaez**

The only thing that's been a worse flop than the organization of nonviolence has been the organization of violence. —**JoanBaez**

If it's natural to kill, how come men have to go into training to learn how?
—**JoanBaez**

The point of nonviolence is to build a floor, a strong new floor, beneath which we can no longer sink. A platform which stands a few feet above napalm, torture, exploitation, poison gas, A and H bombs, the works. Give man a decent place tostand.
—**JoanBaez**

There have been periods of history in which episodes of terrible violence occurred but for which the word violence was never used. . . Violence is shrouded in justifying myths that lend it moral legitimacy, and these myths for the most part kept people from recognizing the violence for what it was. The people who burned witches at the stake never for one moment thought of their act as violence; rather they thought of it as an act of divinely mandated righteousness. The same can be said of most of the violence we humans have evercommitted.
—**GilBailie**

The earth is but one country and mankind itscitizens.
—**Baha'ullah**

The problems of this world are so gigantic that some are paralyzed by their own uncertainty. Courage and wisdom are needed to reach out above this sense of helplessness. Desire for vengeance against deeds of hatred offers no solution. An eye for an eye makes the world blind. If we wish to choose the other path, we will have to search for ways to break the spiral of animosity. To fight evil one must also recognize one's own responsibility. The values for which we stand must be expressed in the way we think of, and how we deal with, our fellowhumans.
—**HM Queen Beatrix of the Netherlands**

The fragrance always remains in the hand that gives therose.
—**HedaBejar**

The finger pulls the trigger, but the trigger may also be pulling the finger.
—**Dr. LeonardBerkowitz**

The God of life summons us to life; more, to be life givers, especially toward those who lie under the heel of thepowers.

—**Daniel Berrigan**

The good thing about Nigeria-phobia is that it may move the current victims to an economic and political Nigerian revolution just like anti-Semitism has made the Jews unresolved in fighting for their own recognition as in this global village. (**EMMANUELADETULA**)

You hate someone, a nation, or a certain people of ethnic origin who are easily recognized because their accents contain foreign or ethnic words pronounced differently from your own acceptable standard, particularly whentheychoosetoliveinacommunitywhereyouareanatural-born citizen, which has now made the true meaning of anti-Semitism as nothing more or less than being anti-accents. **(EMMANUELADETULA)**

The genocide of one million Jews or their experience in the concentration camp of the Nazis sixty years ago should not be something that should receive crocodile tears more than the African genocide where eight hundred thousand African men, women, and children were massacred within ten days, not more than the forty million Africans with HIV/AIDS, or more than the millions without good, hygienic drinking water or food around the world. There is no genocide that the Jews experienced in world history that has not been experienced by other races—if not more genocide, at least not less painful in experience in comparison to the African American race, who has experienced slavery, the experience of the Jews with Nazis can no longer be acceptable as a political tool to justify the pain of the Palestinians in the hand of Israel in the new world order that is in the making. **(EMMANUELADETULA)**

We are all anti-something. Somebody is anti-Tula right now, so the time for the Arab-Israel conflict resolution is now. The time has come for the world to move forward into the next phase of a new world order, and let us come together and establishes the government of peace on earth. **(EMMANUELADETULA-2011)**

Nothing could be worse than the fear that one had given up too soon, and left one unexpended effort that might have saved theworld.
—**JaneAddams**

It is easier to fight for one's principles than to live up tothem.
—**AlfredAdler**

In every child who is born, no matter what circumstances, and of no matter what parents, the potentiality of the human race is born again: and in him, too, once more, and of each of us, our terrific

responsibility toward human life; toward the utmost idea of goodness, of the horror of terror, and ofGod.
—JamesAgee

Let us plant dates even though those who plant them will never eat them. We must live by the love of what we will never see. This is the secret discipline. It is a refusal to let the creative act is dissolved away in immediate sense experience, and a stubborn commitment to the future of our grandchildren. Such disciplined love is what has given prophets, revolutionaries, and saints the courage to die for the future they envisaged. They make their own bodies the seed of their highesthope.
—RubenAlves

We cannot change the past, but we can change our attitude toward it. Uproot guilt and plant forgiveness. Tear out arrogance and seed humility. Exchange love for hate—thereby, making the present comfortable and the futurepromising.
—MayaAngelou

There is no trust more sacred than the one the world holds with children. There is no duty more important than ensuring that their rights are respected, that their welfare is protected, that their lives are free from fear and want and that they grow up inpeace.
—Kofi A. Annan, secretary-general of the UnitedNations

If you see well in people, you radiate a harmonious loving energy which uplifts those who are around you. If you can maintain this habit, this energy will turn into a steady flow oflove.
—AnnamalaiSwami

Peace begins when the hungry are fed. Anger is an acid that can do more harm to the vessel in which it stands than to anything on which it ispoured.

In the struggle rewards are few. In the fact, I know of only two, loving friends and living dreams. These rewards are not so few it seems.

Peace is the work of justice indirectly, in so far as justice removes the obstacles to peace; but it is the work of charity (love) directly, since charity, according to its very notion, causespeace.
—**ThomasAquinas**

Sometime in your life, hope that you might see one starved man, the look on his face when the bread finally arrives. Hope that you might have baked it or bought or even kneaded it yourself. For that look on his face, for your meeting his eyes across a piece of bread, you might be willing to lose a lot, or suffer a lot, or die a little,even.
—**DanielBerrigan**

The human mind likes a strange idea as little as the body likes a strange protein and resists it with a similarenergy.
—**W. H. Beveridge, Britisheconomist**

The most potent weapon in the hands of the oppressor is the mind of theoppressed.
—**SteveBiko**

Can I see another's woe, and not be in sorrow too?
Can I see another's grief, and not seek for kindrelief?
—**WilliamBlake**

To see the world in a grain of sand and heaven in a wild flower, hold infinity in the palm of your hand and eternity in anhour.
—**WilliamBlake**

Joy is the most infallible sign of the presence ofGod.
—**LeonBloy**

When you're finally up on the moon, looking back at the earth, all these differences and nationalistic traits are pretty well going to blend and you're going to get a concept that maybe this is really one

world and why the hell can't we learn to live together like decent people?
—**FrankBorman**

There is no time left for anything but to make peace work a dimension of our every wakingactivity.
—**EliseBoulding**

We do not inherit the earth from our fathers. We borrow it from our children.
—**DavidBower**

Violence in the voice is often only the death rattle of reason in the throat.
—**JohnBoyes**

We have grasped the mystery of the atom and rejected the Sermon on the Mount. Ours is a world of nuclear giants and ethical infants. We know more about war than we know about peace, more about killing that we know aboutliving.
—**Gen. OmarBradley**

The pens which write against disarmament are made with the same steel from which guns aremade.
—**Aristide Briand, French statesman, Nobel Peace Prize winner, 1926**

The pacifist's task today is to find a method of helping and healing which provides a revolutionary constructive substitute forwar.
—**VeraBrittain**

In separateness lies the world's great misery; in compassion lies the world's truestrength.
—**Buddha**

He who can control his rising anger as a coachman controls his carriage at full speed, this man I call a good driver; others merely hold thereins.
—**Buddha**

Your life and my life flow into each other as wave flows into wave, and unless there is peace and joy and freedom for you, there can be no real peace or joy or freedom for me. To see reality—not as we expect it to be but as it is—is to see that unless we live for each other and in and through each other, we do not really live very satisfactorily; that there can really be life only where there really is, in just this sense,love.

—(Carl) FrederickBuechner

[T]o live not with hands clenched to grasp, to strike, to hold tight to a life that is always slipping away the more tightly we hold it, but . . . to live with the hands stretched out both to give and receive with gladness.

—(Carl) FrederickBuechner

The hottest fires in hell are reserved for those who remain neutral in times of moralcrisis.

—EdmundBurke

When you give food to the poor, they call you a saint. When you ask why the poor have no food, they call you acommunist.

—Archbishop Helder Camara, Brazilian liberationtheologist

It is the job of thinking people, not to be on the side of the executioners.

—AlbertCamus

We used to wonder where war lived, what it was that made it so vile. And now we realize that we know where it lives, that it is inside ourselves.

—AlbertCamus

Until we have the courage to recognize cruelty for what it is—whether its victim is human or animal—we cannot expect things to be much better in this world . . . We cannot have peace among men whose hearts delight in killing any living creature. By every act that

glorifies or even tolerates such moronic delight in killing we set back the progress ofhumanity.
—**RachelCarson**

Each person has inside a basic decency and goodness. If he listens to it and acts on it, he is giving a great deal of what it is the world needs most. It is not complicated but it takes courage. It takes courage for a person to listen to his own goodness and act onit.
—**PabloCasals**

In all of his suffering, as in all of his life and ministry, Jesus refused to defend himself with force or with violence. He endured violence and cruelty so that God's love might be fully manifest and the world might be reconciled to the One from whom it had become estranged. Even at his death, Jesus cried for forgiveness for those who were executioners: "Father, forgivethem."
—**"The Challenge ofPeace"**

We look forward to the time when the power to love will replace the love of power. Then will our world know the blessings ofpeace.
—**William ElleryChanning**

Angels can fly because they take themselves solightly.
—**G. K.Chesterton**

If we do not change our direction we are likely to end up where we are headedfor.
—**Chineseproverb**

The question is not, do we go to church; the question is, have we been converted. The crux of Christianity is not whether or not we give donations to popular charities but whether or not we are really committed to thepoor.
—**JoanChittester**

Sports play a societal role in engendering jingoist and chauvinist attitudes. They're designed to organize a community to be committed to theirgladiators.
—**NoamChomsky**

The miracle of the wicked is reinforced by the weakness of the virtuous.
—**WinstonChurchill**

Courage is what it takes to stand up and speak. Courage is also what it takes to sit down andlisten.
—**WinstonChurchill**

I have great belief in the fact that whenever there is chaos, it creates wonderful thinking. I consider chaos agift.
—**Septima PoinsetteClark**

War is an act of violence pushed to its utmostlimits.
—**Maj. General Carl vonClausewitz**

The cause of violence is not ignorance. It is self-interest . . . Only reverence can restrain violence—reverence for human life and the environment.
—**Rev. William Sloan CoffinJr.**

A spiritual person tries less to be godly than to be deeplyhuman.
—**Rev. William Sloan CoffinJr.**

I believe we are on the edge of a quantum leap into a whole new way of organizing and living as a humanfamily.
—**Mairead CorriganMaguire**

War is an invention of the human mind. The human mind can invent peace withjustice.
—**NormanCousins**

The idea of absolute freedom is fiction. It's based on the idea of an independent self. But, in fact, there's no such thing. There's no self without other people. There's no self without sunlight. There's no self without dew. And water. And bees to pollinate the food we eat .

. . So the idea of behaving in a way that doesn't acknowledge those reciprocal relationships is not really freedom, itsindulgence.
—**PeterCoyote**

We are, each of us angels with only one wing; and we can only fly by embracing oneanother.
—**Luciano deCrescenzo**

No one is so foolish as to prefer to peace, war, in which, instead of sons burying their fathers, fathers bury theirsons.
—**Croesus, king of Lydia, in Herodotus's *The PersianWars***

Truly man is the king of beasts, for his brutality exceeds them. We live by the death of others. We are burial places! I have from an early age abjured the use of meat, and the time will come when men such as I will look upon the murder of animals as they now look on the murder ofmen.
—**Leonardo daVinci**

It is penance to work, to give oneself to others, to endure the pinpricks of communityliving.
—**DorothyDay**

An act of love, a voluntary taking on oneself of some of the pain of the world, increases the courage and love and hope ofall.
—**DorothyDay**

No one has a right to sit down and feel hopeless. There is too much work todo.
—**DorothyDay**

We plant seeds that will flower as results in our lives, so best to remove the weeds of anger, avarice, envy and doubt that peace and abundance may manifest forall.
—**DorothyDay**

Young people say, What is the sense of our small effort? They cannot see that we must lay one brick at time, take one step at a time; we can be responsible only for the one action in the presentmoment.

But we can beg for an increase of love in our hearts that will vitalize and transform all our individual actions, and know that God will take them and multiply them, as Jesus multiplied the loaves andfishes.
—**DorothyDay**

If you want to make peace, you don't talk to your friends. You talk to yourenemies.
—**MosheDayan**

Someday, after we have mastered the winds, the waves, the tides and gravity, shall harness for God the energies of love. Then for the second time in the history of the world, we will have discoveredfire.
—**Teilhard deChardin**

War stirs in men's hearts the mud of their worst instincts. It puts a premium on violence, nourishes hatred, and gives free rein to cupidity. It crushes the weak, exalts the unworthy, and bolsters tyranny . . . Time and time again it has destroyed all ordered living, devastated hope, and put the prophets todeath.
—**Charles deGaulle**

Nobody was born nonviolent. No one was born charitable. None of us comes to these things by nature but only by conversion. The first duty of the nonviolent community is helping its members work upon themselves and come toconversion.
—**Lanza delVasto**

The longer we listen to one another—with real attention—the more commonality we will find in all our lives. That is, if we are careful to exchange with one another life stories and not simplyopinions.
—**BarbaraDeming**

Gandhi once declared that it was his wife who unwittingly taught him the effectiveness of nonviolence. Who better than women should know that battles can be won without resort to physical strength? Who better than we should know all the power that resides innoncooperation?

-**BarbaraDeming**

What is the revolution that we need? We need to dissolve the lie that some people have a right to think of other people as their property. And we need at last to form a circle that includes us all, in which all of us are seen as equal . . . We do not belong to the other, but our lives are linked; we belong in a circle ofothers.
—**BarbaraDeming**

To resort to power one need not be violent, and to speak to conscience one need not be meek. The most effective action both resorts to power and engages conscience. Nonviolent actions do not have to get others to be nice. It can in effect force them to consult their consciences. Nor does it have to petition those in power to do something about a situation. It can face the authorities with a new fact and say: Accept this new situation which we havecreated.
—**BarbaraDeming**

Love the fellow of the resurrection, scooping up the dust and chanting"Live!"
—**EmilyDickinson**

Abba Poeman said about Abba Prior that every single day he made a freshbeginning.
—**Desert Fathers andMothers**

Justice is truth inaction.
—**BenjaminDisraeli**

At some ideas you stand perplexed, especially at the sight of human sins, uncertain whether to combat it by force or by human love. Always decide, "I will combat it with human love." If you make up your mind about that once and for all, you can conquer the whole world. Loving humility is a terrible force; it is the strongest of all things and there is nothing likeit.
—**Dostoyevsky's** *The BrothersKaramazov*

The first thing to be disrupted by our commitment to nonviolence will be not the system but our ownlives.

—**JamesDouglass**

Mankind will never win lasting peace so long as men use their full resources only in tasks of war. While we are yet at peace, let us mobilize the potentialities, particularly the moral and spiritual potentialities, which we usually reserve forwar.

—John Foster Dulles's *War or Peace*(1950)

Those for whom peace is no more than a dream are asleep to the future.

—JackDuVall

What good is it to me that Mary gave birth to the son of God fourteen hundred years ago, and I do not also give birth to the Son of God in my time and in my culture? We are all meant to be mothers of God. God always needs to beborn.

—MeisterEckhart

The pioneers of a warless world are the young men (and women) who refuse militaryservice.

—AlbertEinstein

We must be prepared to make heroic sacrifices for the cause of peace that we make ungrudgingly for the cause of war. There is no task that is more important or closer to myheart.

—AlbertEinstein

Out of clutter finds simplicity. From discord, find harmony. In the middle of difficulty, liesopportunity.

—AlbertEinstein

Whatever you do, you need courage. Whatever course you decide upon, there is always someone to tell you that you are wrong. There are always difficulties arising that tempt you to believe your critics are right. To map out a course of action and follow it to an end requires some of the same courage that a soldier needs. Peace has its victories, but it takes brave men and women to winthem.

—Ralph WaldoEmerson

Every gun that is made, every warship launched, every rocket fired signifies, in the final sense, a theft from those who hunger and are not fed, those who are cold and are notclothed.
—**Dwight D. Eisenhower(1890–1969)**

I know not with what weapons World War III will be fought, but World War IV will be fought with sticks andstones.
—**AlbertEinstein**

Non-violence leads to the highest ethics, which is the goal of all evolution. Until we stop harming all other living beings, we are still savages.
—**ThomasEdison**

There will one day spring from the brain of science a machine or force so fearful in its potentialities, so absolutely terrifying, that even man, the fighter, who will dare torture and death in order to inflict torture and death, will be appalled, and so abandon warforever.
—**ThomasEdison**

Any intelligent fool can make things bigger, more complex, and more violent. It takes a touch of genius—and a lot of courage—to move in the oppositedirection.
—**AlbertEinstein**

When death, the great reconciler, has come; it is never our tenderness that we repent of, but ourseverity.
—**GeorgeEliot**

There is nothing that war has ever achieved that we could not better achieve withoutit.
—**HavelockEllis**

Some things you must always be unable to bear. Some things you must never stop refusing to bear. Injustice and outrage and dishonor and shame. No matter how young you are or how old you have got.

Not for kudos and not for cash, your picture in the paper nor money in the bank, neither. Just refuse to bearthem.
—**WilliamFaulkner**

The absence of risk is a sure sign ofmediocrity.
—**Charles deFoucauld**

The law, in its majestic equality, forbids both rich and poor to sleep under bridges, to beg in the streets, and to stealbread.
—**Anatole-France**

While you are proclaiming peace with your lips is careful to have it even more fully in yourheart.
—**St. Francis ofAssisi**

Not to hurt our humble brethren (the animals) is our first duty to them, but to stop there is not enough. We have a higher mission—to be of service to them whenever they require it . . . If you have men who will exclude any of God's creatures from the shelter of compassion and pity, you will have men who will deal likewise with their fellowmen.
—**St. Francis ofAssisi**

Nothing is as strong as gentleness; nothing so gentle as realstrength.
—**St. Francis deSales**

I resolve to speak ill of no man whatever, not even in a matter of truth; but rather by some means excuse the faults I hear charged upon others, and upon proper occasions speak all the good I know of everybody.
—**BenjaminFranklin**

Productive work, love and thought are possible only if a person can be, when necessary, quiet and alone. To be able to listen to one is the necessary condition for relating oneself toothers.
—**ErichFromm**

We are going to have to find ways of organizing ourselves cooperatively, sanely, scientifically, harmonically and in regenerative spontaneity with the rest of humanity around the earth . . . We are not going to be able to operate our spaceship earth successfully nor for much longer unless we see it as a whole spaceship and our fate ascommon.
—**BuckminsterFuller**

Change comes not from men and women changing their minds, but from the change from one generation to thenext.
—**J. K.Galbraith**

Peace we want because there is another war to fight against poverty, disease andignorance.
—**Indira Gandhi,1966**

I claim to be no more than an average person with less than average ability. I have not the shadow of doubt that any man or woman can achieve what I have, if he or she would make the same effort and cultivate the same hope andfaith.
—**MohandasGandhi**

Nonviolence which is a quality of the heart cannot come by an appeal to thebrain.
—**MahatmaGandhi**

We must be the change we wish tosee.
—**MahatmaGandhi**

We may never be strong enough to be entirely nonviolent in thought, word and deed. But we must keep nonviolence as our goal and make strong progress towards it. The Attainment of freedom, whether for a person, a nation or a world, must be in exact proportion to the attainment of nonviolence foreach.
—**MohandasGandhi**

Nonviolence is not a garment to be put on and off at will. Its seat is in the heart, and it must be an inseparable part of ourbeing.
—**MahatmaGandhi**

I am part and parcel of the whole and cannot find God apart from the rest ofhumanity.
—**MohandasGandhi**

Whenever you are in doubt or when the self becomes too much with you, try the following experiment: Recall the face of the poorest and most helpless person you have ever seen and ask yourself if the step you contemplate is going to be for any use to him or to her . . . Then you will find your doubts and your self-meltingaway.
—**MohandasGandhi**

It is easier to lead men to combat, stirring up their passion, than to restrain them and direct them toward the patient labors ofpeace.
—**AndreGide**

Believe those who are seeking the truth; doubt those who findit.
—**AndreGide**

The gloom of the world is but a shadow. Behind it, yet within reach, is joy. There is radiance and glory in the darkness, could we but see, and to see, we have only to look. I beseech you tolook.
Fra Giovanni,1513

Beneath the rule of men entirely great. The pen is mightier than the sword.
—**Edward GeorgeBulwer-Lytton**

Better than a thousand hollow words, Is one word that bringspeace.
—**Buddha**

There are three truths: my truth, your truth and thetruth.
—**Chineseproverb**

You cannot shake hands with a clenchedfist.
—**Indira Gandhi,1971**

I hope . . . that mankind will at length, as they call themselves reasonable creatures, have reason and sense enough to settle their differences without cutting throats; for in my opinion there never was a good war, or a bad peace.
—**Benjamin Franklin**

A peace that comes from fear and not from the heart is the opposite of peace.
—**Gersonides**

Our friends show us what we can do; our enemies teach us what we must do.
—**Goethe**

When I despair, I remember that all through history the way of truth and love has always won. There have been tyrants and murderers and for a time they seem invincible but in the end, they always fall— think of it, ALWAYS!
—**Mahatma Gandhi**

Very few people chose war. They chose selfishness and the result was war. Each of us, individually and nationally, must choose: total love or total war.
—**Dave Dellinger**

Since wars begin in the minds of men, it is in the minds of men that the defenses of peace must be constructed.
—**UNESCO**

Peace is more precious than a piece of land.
—**Anwar Sadat**

The peace makers shall be called the children of God.
—**Bible**

If you want to make peace, you don't talk to your friends. You talk to your enemies.
—**Moshe Dayan**

Every kind of peaceful cooperation among men is primarily based on mutual trust and only secondarily on institutions such as courts of justice andpolice.
—**AlbertEinstein**

Think not forever of yourselves, O Chiefs, nor of your own generation. Think of continuing generations of our families, think of our grandchildren and of those yet unborn, whose faces are coming from beneath theground?
—**T. S.Eliot**

Nothing can bring you peace but yourself; nothing, but the triumph ofprinciples.
—**Ralph WaldoEmerson**

There never was a good war or a badpeace.
—**BenjaminFranklin**

It is easier to lead men to combat, stirring up their passion, than to restrain them and direct them toward the patient labors ofpeace.
—**AndreGide**

Social advance depends as much upon the process through which it is secured as upon the resultitself.
—**JaneAddams**

Peace and friendship with all mankind is our wisest policy, and I wish we may be permitted to pursueit.
—**ThomasJefferson**

Yes, we are all different. Different customs, different foods, different mannerisms, different languages, but not so different that we cannot get along with one another. If we will disagree without being disagreeable.
—**J. MartinKohe**

Peace with a club in hand iswar.
—**Portugueseproverb**

We must build a new world, a far better world—one in which the eternal dignity of man isrespected.
—**Harry S.Truman**

Non-violence leads to the highest ethics, which is the goal of all evolution. Until we stop harming all other living beings, we are still savages.
—**Thomas A.Edison**

They are not following dharma that resort to violence to achieve their purpose. But those who lead others through nonviolent means, knowing right and wrong, may be called guardians of thedharma.
—**Buddha**

Violence does, in truth, recoil upon the violent, and the schemer falls into the pit which he digs foranother.
—**Sir Arthur ConanDoyle**

Violence is the last refuge of theincompetent.
—**SalvorHardin**

Quotes from MahatmaGandhi

A man is the sum of his actions, of what he has done, of what he can do, Nothingelse.

We must become the change we want tosee.

To believe in something, and not to live it, isdishonest.

When I despair, I remember that all through history the way of truth and love has always won. There have been tyrants and murderers and for a time they seem invincible but in the end, they always fall—think of it,ALWAYS.

Non-violence is the article offaith.

It is easy enough to be friendly to one's friends. But to befriend the one who regards himself as your enemy is the quintessence of true religion. The other is merebusiness.

Hatred can be overcome only bylove.

I first learned the concepts of non-violence in my marriage.

Poverty is the worst form ofviolence.

An eye for eye only ends up making the whole world blind.

Unity to be real must stand the severest strain withoutbreaking.

Strength does not come from physical capacity. It comes from an indomitablewill.

Quotes fromBuddha

There has to be evil so that good can prove its purity aboveit.

When one has the feeling of dislike for evil, when one feels tranquil, one finds pleasure in listening to good teachings; when one has these feelings and appreciates them, and one is free offear.

Hatred does not cease by hatred, but only by love; this is the eternal rule.

We are what we think. All that we are arises with our thoughts. With our thoughts, We make ourworld.

Quotes fromLao-tzu

I have three precious things which I hold fast and prize. The first is gentleness; the second is frugality; the third is humility, which keeps me from putting myself before others. Be gentle and you can be bold; be frugal and you can be liberal; avoid putting yourself before others and you can become a leader amongmen.

Nothing in the world is more flexible and yielding than water. Yet when it attacks the firm and the strong, none can withstand it, because they have no way to change it. So the flexible overcome the adamant, the yielding overcome the forceful. Everyone knows this, but no one can doit.

The softest things in the world overcome the hardest things in the world.

Whosesoever's the sun shines, the wind blows, there is an ear to hear, and a mind to conceive, there let the precepts of life be made known, let the maxims of truth be honored and obeyed, let there be music, and let there bePeace.
—**Dave Johnston, guitarplayer**

If we suppose a sufficient righteousness and intelligence in men to produce presently, from the tremendous lessons of history, an effective will for a world peace—that is to say, an effective will for a world law under a world government—for in no other fashion is a secure world peace conceivable—in what manner may we expect things to move towards this end? . . . It is an educational task, and its very essence is to bring to the minds of all men everywhere, as a necessary basis for world cooperation, a new telling and interpretation, a common interpretation, ofhistory.
—**H. G.Wells**

Whenever there is any feeling of tension or discord, I discovered that if I looked within myself for the fault and did not blame the other person, then tension and discordceased.
—**Gandhi**

Imagine all the people living in peace. You may say I'm a dreamer, but I'm not the only one. I hope someday you'll join us, and the world will live asone.
—JohnLennon

Every gun that is made, every warship launched, every rocket fired signifies, in the final sense, a theft from those who hunger and are not fed, those who are cold and are notclothed.
—Dwight D.Eisenhower

Peace cannot be kept by force. It can only be achieved by understanding.
—AlbertEinstein

Courage is the price that life extracts for granting peace. The soul that knows it not, knows no release from little things; Knows not the livid loneliness offear.
—AmeliaEarhart

There is one purpose to life and one only: to bear witness to and understand as much as possible of the complexity of the world—its beauty, its mysteries, its riddles. The more you understand, the more you look, the greater is your enjoyment of life and your sense of peace. That's all there is to it. If an activity is not grounded in "to love" or "to learn," it does not havevalue.
—AnneRice

We make war that we may live inpeace.
—Aristotle

Everything that has a beginning has an ending. Make your peace with that and all will bewell.
—Buddha

Peace comes from within. Do not seek itwithout.
—Buddha

Believe nothing, no matter where you read it, or who said it, no matter if I have said it, unless it agrees with your own reason and your own commonsense.
—Buddha

He who loves 50 people has 50 woes; he who loves no one has no woes.
—Buddha

To be at peace with ourselves we need to knowourselves.
—CaitlinMatthews

The fidelity of the United States to security treaties is not just an empty matter. It is a pillar of peace in theworld.
—David Dean Rusk

The secret to bringing peace to earth is bearing in mind that the world is simply what it is. And is it so small a place, that you could change it radically? Live at peace with yourself, if you would bring peace even to one other humanbeing.
—DonaldWalters

I like to believe that people in the long run are going to do more to promote peace than our governments. Indeed, I think that people want peace so much that one of these days' governments had better get out of the way and let them haveit.
—Dwight D.Eisenhower

Five great enemies to peace inhabit with us: avarice, ambition, envy, anger and pride. If those enemies were to be banished, we should infallibly enjoy perpetualpeace.
—FrancescoPetrarch

Peace does not dwell in outward things, but within the soul; we may preserve it in the midst of the bitterest pain, if our will remains firm and submissive. Peace in this life springs from acquiescence, not in an exemption fromsuffering.
—FrancisFenelon

I do not want the peace which passed understanding; I want the understanding which bringethpeace.
—**HelenKeller**

One of the most basic principles for making and keeping peace within and between nations . . . is that in political, military, moral, and spiritual confrontations, there should be an honest attempt at the reconciliation of differences before resorting tocombat.
—**James Earl CarterJr.**

The white, the Hispanic, the black, the Arab, the Jew, the woman, the Native American, the small farmer, the businessperson, the environmentalist, the peace activist, the young, the old, the lesbian, the gay and the disabled make up the Americanquilt.
—**Jesse LouisJackson**

Those who make peaceful revolution impossible will make violent revolutioninevitable.
—**John FitzgeraldKennedy**

World peace, like community peace, does not require that each man love his neighbor—it requires only that they live together with mutual tolerance, submitting their disputes to a just and peaceful settlement.
—**John FitzgeraldKennedy**

The world will never have lasting peace so long as men reserve for war the finest human qualities. Peace, no less than war, requires idealism and self-sacrifice and a righteous and dynamicfaith.
—**John FosterDulles**

For peace of mind, we need to resign as general manager of the universe.
—**LarryEisenberg**

However vague they are, dreams have a way of concealing themselves and leave us no peace until they are translated into reality, like seeds germinating underground, sure to sprout in their search for thesunlight.
—**LinYutang**

Peace is such a precious jewel that I would give anything for it but truth.
—**MatthewHenry**

I offer you peace. I offer you love. I offer you friendship. I see your beauty. I hear your need. I feel your feelings. My wisdom flows from the Highest Source. I salute that Source in you. Let us work together for unity andlove.
—**MohandasGandhi**

The greatest destroyer of peace is abortion because if a mother can kill her own child, what is left for me to kill you and you to kill me? There is nothingbetween.
—**MotherTeresa**

Is life so dear, or peace so sweet, as to be purchased at the price of chains or slavery? Forbid it, Almighty God! I know not what course others may take but as for me; give me liberty or give medeath!
—**PatrickHenry**

Even a fool, when he holdeth his peace, is counted wise: and he that shutteth his lips is esteemed a man ofunderstanding.
—**Proverbs17:28**

But all who humble themselves before the Lord shall be given every blessing and shall have wonderfulpeace.
—**Psalm 37:11 (The LivingBible)**

You can't make war in the Middle East without Egypt and you can't make peace withoutSyria.
—**Robert F.Kennedy**

Never continue in a job you don't enjoy. If you're happy in what you're doing, you'll like yourself, you'll have inner peace. And if you have that, along with physical health, you will have had more success than you could possibly haveimagined.
—**Rodan ofAlexandria**

I call upon the scientific community in our country, those who gave us nuclear weapons, to turn their great talents now to the cause of mankind and world peace: to give us the means of rendering these nuclear weapons impotent andobsolete.
—**Ronald WilsonReagan**

The vote on the Peacekeeper is also a vote on Geneva. Rejecting the Peacekeeper will knock the legs out from under the   negotiating table.
—**Ronald Wilson Reagan on the importance of the MXmissile**

Lord, make me an instrument of your peace; where there is hatred, let me sow love; where there is injury, pardon; where there is doubt, faith; where there is despair, hope; where there is darkness, light; and where there is sadness,joy.
—**St.Augustine**

If ye love wealth greater than liberty, the tranquility of servitude greater than the animating contest for freedom, go home from us in peace. We seek not your counsel, nor your arms. Crouch down and lick the hand that feeds you. May your chains set lightly upon you; and may posterity forget that ye were ourcountrymen.
—**SamuelAdams**

The said constitution shall never be construed to authorize congress to prevent the people of the United States who are peaceable citizens from keeping their own arms The deepest American dream is not the hunger for money or fame; it is the dream of settling down, in peace and freedom and cooperation, in the promisedland.
—**Scott RussellSanders**

We can never obtain peace in the world if we neglect the inner world and don't make peace with ourselves. World peace must develop out of innerpeace.
—**the DalaiLama**

The book is here to stay. What we're doing is symbolic of the peaceful coexistence of the book and thecomputer.
—**VartanGregorian**

Peace and war begin at home. If we truly want peace in the world, let us begin by loving one another in our own families. If we want to spread joy, we need for every family to havejoy.
—**MotherTeresa**

Do everything with a mind that lets go. Don't accept praise or gain or anything else. If you let go a little you will have a little peace; if you let go a lot you will have a lot of peace; if you let go completely you will have completepeace.
—**AjahnChah**

Maybe we should develop a Crayola bomb as our next secret weapon. A happiness weapon. A beauty bomb. And every time a crisis developed, we would launch one. It would explode high in the air—explode softly—and send thousands, millions, of little parachutes into the air. Floating down to earth—boxes of Crayolas. And we wouldn't go cheap, either—not little boxes of eight. Boxes of sixty-four, with the sharpener built right in. With silver and gold and copper, magenta and peach and lime, amber and umber and all the rest. And people would smile and get a little funny look on their faces and cover the world with theirimagination.
—**RobertFulghum**

If civilization is to survive, we must cultivate the science of human relationships—the ability of all peoples, of all kinds, to live together, in the same world atpeace.
—**Franklin D.Roosevelt**

Those who make peaceful revolution impossible will make violent revolutioninevitable.
—**John FitzgeraldKennedy**

Realize that true happiness lies within you. Waste no time and effort searching for peace and contentment and joy in the world outside. Remember that there is no happiness in having or in getting, but only in giving. Reach out. Share. Smile. Hug. Happiness is a perfume you cannot pour on others without getting a few drops onyourself.
—OgMandino

If there must be trouble let it be in my day, that my child may have peace.
—ThomasPaine

Whatever you do, you need courage. Whatever course you decide upon, there is always someone to tell you that you are wrong. There are always difficulties arising that tempt you to believe your critics are right. To map out a course of action and follow it to an end requires some of the same courage that a soldier needs. Peace has its victories, but it takes brave men and women to winthem.
—Ralph WaldoEmerson

Franklin D.Roosevelt

CONTACT THEAUTHOR&PUBLISHER

Dr. Emmanuel Adetula
TULATAX Office

Dr. Emmanuel Adetula
YAHUTULA MEDICAL
TULALUM HOUSE
Lagos/Ibadan Expressway
Olomi-Academy, Ibadan
Oyo State-Nigeria
www.yahumedical.org
yahumedical@gmail.com

1354 w 84th Place
Los Angeles, CA. 90044
(310) 292-1147
tulatax2015@gmail.com
www.emmanueltula.com

File Your Taxes Free Online!
TULATAX
www.tulatax.com
MOBILE NOTARY PUBLIC
PICK-UP AND DELIVERY SERVICE

For wholesale copy price of this book, Please write to:
Emmanuel Adetula Christ Channel Network
P.O. BOX 1017 Lawndale, CA. 90260 USA
Order your copy today at www.amazon.com

www.ingramcontent.com/pod-product-compliance
Lightning Source LLC
Chambersburg PA
CBHW060656280326
41933CB00012B/2211